# Handbook of Religious Services

Church of the Larger Fellowship,
Boston, Massachusetts.

Originally edited by Dr. George N. Marshall and published in 1967
as the *Service Handbook for CLF Members*, this new edition has
been edited by Rev. Scott W. Alexander, Rev. O. Eugene Pickett,
Helen Pickett, Joan Goodwin, and Nancy Engels.

# Dedication

Dr. George N. Marshall
Minister, Church of the Larger Fellowship
1960-1985

Dr. Marshall's leadership established CLF as a
congregation with a unique role to play in the
Unitarian Universalist movement.

# Foreword

This *Handbook of Religious Services* is a major revision of the
Service Handbook first published by the Church of the Larger
Fellowship in 1967. The Reverend Dr. George N.
Marshall, minister
of CLF for 25 years, was its first editor and was responsible for its
subsequent revision. In the first edition Dr.
Marshall wrote, "The
scattered members of the CLF often find themselves alone when
facing the great issues of life—the dedication of children, the
marriage of young people and adults, the final arrangements which
come with death.... When we mourn, or when we rejoice, we want to
be true to our ideals and our beliefs, and accordingly have services
which express them.... The suggestions and services are arranged
with our isolated families in mind." The Service Handbook has
served our members well and has been used by thousands of
Unitarian Universalists.

This new edition, *Handbook of Religious Services*, is designed to be
helpful to individuals and families in facing "the great issues of life"
and has been expanded to encourage family worship and to serve as
a resource for small groups and congregations. We feel that this new
book will enhance CLF's mission, not only to minister to isolated
Unitarian Universalists, but also to strengthen and extend our larger
Unitarian Universalist movement.

We have drawn upon the writings and works of many Unitarian
Universalists in order to reflect the diverse and pluralistic nature of
our liberal religious Association. We have attempted to identify the
sources of all quoted materials. If we have not given proper credit,
we apologize. These services and readings may be adapted to make
them more appropriate for your individual or group use.

I would like to give special thanks to the Reverend Scott Alexander,
who had the major responsibility for compiling material for this new
edition, and to Nancy Engels, who was responsible for the design
and production of the book. In addition, the rest of us on the CLF
staff—Joan Goodwin, Helen Pickett, and I—have contributed signifi-
cantly to its planning, development, and publication. Since this was
a collaborative effort, all of us can be named as editors. The handbook has been funded in part by the Unitarian Universalist Denom-
inational Grants Panel.

We hope this new *Handbook of Religious Services* will enrich the
religious lives of all who use it.

*Eugene Pickett, Minister*
*Summer 1990*

# Table of Contents

# How to Use This Handbook

The *Handbook of Religious Services* has been designed to help you plan and conduct simple worship services or special ceremonies within your family, with a small group or congregation, or by yourself.

The first four chapters present information and materials for planning worship services for the family or small gatherings at home, child namings or dedications, weddings, and memorial services.

Each chapter outlines an order of service, proposes specific procedures and materials, and suggests additional resources to consult. A checklist reminds you of steps to complete before your service begins.

In Chapter 5, you will find six collections of readings and meditations from which you may select worship elements appropriate for your services: Opening Words, Chalice or Candle Lighting Words, Meditations and Prayers, Closing Words, Table Graces, and Bedtime Prayers.

For the best planning results, you might develop your own order of service and your own checklist of things to do or gather for each service you plan to conduct. Then make photocopies from this book of the basic service you are using, as well as additional elements you select, so that, without marking your handbook, you may arrange and adapt your selections in the order you plan to use them. Choose options [material within square brackets means you must choose from options or supply names] from the text, and make notations of the names and pronouns to use, so that you will have a complete copy of the service as you plan to present it. If you bind the pages in a paper folder or looseleaf binder, you will be spared extra paper-shuffling at the lectern or site.

With the materials and guidance in this handbook, you should have the confidence to organize and conduct meaningful Unitarian Universalist worship services.

# Chapter One
# Unitarian Universalist Worship

Unitarian Universalist worship is as diverse as it is important. The origin of the word "worship" is in the old English **weorthscippen**, meaning to ascribe worth to something, to shape things of worth. We worship, then, whenever we ascribe worth to some value, idea, object, person, experience, attitude, or activity or whenever we give form or shape to that which we have already found to be of worth.

A worship experience can occur at any time, whether one is alone or part of a group. Whenever something beautiful is perceived, whenever there is a deep sense of connectedness with other persons, with the natural world, or with the transcendent (however defined), whenever one gains insight or a new sense of wholeness, whenever one perceives an ethical challenge, whenever life is deliberately focused or ordered—all of these situations may be considered worship.

When UUs gather for worship, they intend to create some kind of shared and worthwhile experience. A worship service is a deliberate shaping, ordering, or recalling of individual thoughts and experiences, done in the context of a community of persons who share common values, ideas, and attitudes.

Sharing in worship with others helps us declare, celebrate, and affirm what is "of worth" in our lives and the world. To worship is to respond to the religious impulse to give shape and meaning to existence, to be purposeful and positive as citizens of Earth.

And the good news is that there is no great secret about how to create and conduct meaningful and satisfying worship! Many religious liberals mistakenly think that some mysterious "expertise" is required in order to be a worship planner or leader. They cannot imagine themselves capable of planning a worship experience that others will find rewarding and meaningful. While effective worship does require thoughtful and careful planning, it is not some lofty and difficult mystery. If we hesitate to offer our humanness through the form of worship, we miss an important opportunity to engage and improve our world.

# Group Worship

Just as important as the content of any worship service is the setting that the worship leader(s) create. Many non-verbal dimensions of the worship experience can directly affect the quality of the service. First, arrange whatever space is being used to ensure that it looks and feels like "sacred" space—space that reflects the worth and beauty of what is being celebrated, cherished, affirmed, or embraced. Here are a few details that deserve attention:

**First Impressions Are Important**  Is the worship space clean, neat, and cared for? Is it bright, welcoming, and ready for the important business at hand? Are the chairs and other furniture thoughtfully and pleasingly arranged? Have extraneous objects been put away? Is the lighting comfortable? (Sometimes softening the lighting just as the service begins is very effective.) Does the worship space reflect the care and concern you have for your Unitarian Universalist faith? A little attention to such physical details can make a world of difference!

**Starting on Time**  Some UU groups use a gentle gong or bell or soft prelude music to let people know that the service is about to begin and that it is time for them to take their seats and prepare themselves for worship. Beginning on time reduces the discomfort of visitors and communicates to everyone that you are well organized and serious about the service that is to take place.

**Order of Service**  Provide an Order of Service for participants to follow. It can be printed ahead of time and handed out, or posted in front of the group. A printed order of service helps participants to relax, because they know that they do not have to worry about being surprised or confused during the service. If the group regularly recites or sings something together, make sure the words are printed for visitors.

**Greenery or Flowers**  Live plants or flower arrangements can add greatly to an atmosphere of peace, reflection, serenity, and beauty. Place them carefully to complement other worship-space objects (chalice, symbols, banners).

**A Focal Point**  When you arrange the room to draw attention to a central point—perhaps adjacent to a podium, lectern, or pulpit—you enhance the experience of comfort, community, inspiration, and sense of purpose that shared worship can bring.

**Art Objects, Symbols, Decorations**  Drawing attention to a single object, symbol, or decoration helps people to focus on the matter at hand. Simplicity is usually the key to effective use of flowers, paintings, sculptures, or banners. One large piece, centrally located, is often more effective than several small pieces. If possible, find an object that is related to the day's theme; it can be enjoyed in itself and provide reinforcement for the theme in symbolic form.

Symbols are particularly well suited to worship because they invite viewers to ponder their personal responses.

**The Flame of Fellowship** Lighting a candle or chalice at the start of a service, when repeated week after week, can become a powerful and meaningful symbol to focus group worship. You may do this with or without spoken words. (Several examples can be found on pages 54-55.)

**Audio-visuals** Technical problems with audio-visual equipment can disrupt a service and distract a congregation. If you use projectors, tape recorders, video equipment, or microphones, set them up and check them out beforehand. If possible, have someone other than the worship leader operate the machines, and do a complete technical rehearsal in the meeting room with that person.

**Music** Music can bring about religious and spiritual experiences that words cannot. Music evokes moods of celebration and contemplation, amplifying and intensifying the spoken word. Live music has excitement and immediacy, but recorded music (if carefully selected and skillfully presented) can also be effective. Music in a service should complement what has gone before and lead into what happens next. Choir and congregational singing invite active participation in the service.

**Congregational Participation** Merely by their presence, individuals who come to worship are participating. In addition, participation can be formalized by: hymns, unison and responsive readings, and affirmations; sharing announcements, personal joys, concerns, and prayers; a feedback time after the sermon or presentation, or questions and dialogue structured right into the service. As a rule, some structured participation enriches worship for the congregation, but services can be effective without it. Varying the forms of congregational participation can help prevent "staleness" and offer additional levels of engagement for those who attend.

## Putting the Service Together
Spend some time identifying and focussing on the theme of your service. Perhaps there is a seasonal holiday, an event of significance in the community, an ethical, political, or religious controversy, or a personal perspective you wish to address. A clear focus is essential.

**Outline** Make an outline of the components you envision in your service. The four Orders of Service that follow may help you design your overall approach.

Here are several examples of simple orders of service:
*A few moments with the children for a story or talk could be added early in any service.*

## Service A
Musical Prelude
Opening Words
Hymn or Song
Chalice or Candle Lighting
Joys, Concerns,
    Announcements
Reading or Meditation
Musical Interlude
    *an offering may be taken*
    *at this time*
Sermon
Discussion of Sermon
    *(optional)*
Hymn or Song
Closing Words
Musical Postlude

## Service B
Welcome and
    Announcements
Joys and Concerns
Prelude Music
Chalice or Candle Lighting
Hymn
Reading(s)
Silent or Spoken Meditation
Offertory
Sermon
Musical Meditation
Benediction

## Service C
Welcome
Music
Reading
Music or Silent Meditation
Sermon
Discussion *(optional)*
Music
Closing Words

## Service D
Opening Words
Chalice or Candle Lighting
Silent Meditation
Sermon or Address
Discussion *(optional)*
Closing Words

**Gather Materials**  With a general plan in mind, locate readings, meditations, music, and other elements that you feel enrich your theme or focus. You will find a variety of good materials in Chapter 5 of this handbook. You or members of your group may have other favorites you wish to incorporate. The Unitarian Universalist Association publishes several worship aids that are available through the UUA Bookstore at 25 Beacon Street, Boston, MA 02108.

Especially helpful for small groups are:

*Readings for Common Worship*, Paperback, published by the UUA, 1981 (a collection of modern responsive readings).

*Leading Congregations in Worship—A Guide*, Paperback, published by the UUA, 1983 (many suggestions and service components).

*Hymns in New Form for Common Worship*, Paperback, published by the UUA, 1982 (favorite hymns in gender-inclusive, non-patriarchal language).

A comprehensive new UUA hymnbook is being published as this handbook goes to press.

**Prepare Service Copy** Make copies of your selected materials (including the ones from this handbook) so that you can edit them and arrange them in the order in which you will present them. You might write instructions to yourself in a different-colored ink, or make extra copies for other participants to use. *(Brackets in the material [ ] indicate places in the service where you must choose from proposed options or fill in names.)*

**Finally** When you have the whole service organized, read it through carefully, noting any special materials you may need to have on hand (candles, lighters, flowers), or people who must be contacted to take part (pianist, ushers). Practice speaking the service at a slow, measured pace—people not trained as public speakers often speak much too rapidly. Ask someone to listen and comment on your delivery.

Review the "Setting the Stage" steps, plan for your focal point, and decide whether to print an order of service. Make a checklist of all the things that must be taken care of by you or someone else before the service begins. Do them!

Tending to these details goes a long way toward ensuring a rewarding experience for everyone involved. Now you are ready! Take a deep breath and proceed.

## Family Worship

Some two hundred years ago, when Unitarianism and Universalism were new in North America, prayers were part of the family's daily ritual. Gradually, we have let go of this practice. Though some UU families still say grace at meals or encourage children to say bedtime prayers, even these simple customs have been largely abandoned.

Some form of religious observance—call it worship, celebration, or what you will—is necessary to our spiritual growth whether we're part of a congregation or not. We may worship, celebrate, sing, and meditate by ourselves when we feel the need. We may also create opportunities to do these things together as a family in our own home, whether or not we belong to a congregation.

As Corita Kent wrote:

> *In trying to get hold of things mysterious*
> *we try to invent something definite*
> *and mystery can never be defined*
> *or must always be redefined*
> *or better yet*
> *come at newly and indirectly*
> *through stories and things around us*

> *thru parables and food ... with the ordinary everyday people
> and stuff around us.*

Jews have strengthened their faith through centuries of Diaspora, or wide dispersal, by means of home observances: lighting Sabbath candles at the dinner table, celebrating Passover with a ceremonial family meal, reliving the great story of the eight days of Hanukkah.

How can UU families, despite the hectic pace of our lives, create our own occasions for getting hold of the mystery, using "the ordinary everyday people and stuff around us"?

The Rev. Robert L'H. Miller, former member of CLF's religious education committee, has written:

> *The stuff of your daily life experience and its language and style of expression should provide content and context for family celebrations. Our celebrations affirm our beliefs in the goodness of life, the supreme worth of persons, the creative process of sharing, the search for truth. Our celebrations clarify our values and help us to learn what is good, what kind of person am I, what kind of persons are others? Our celebrations enhance our feeling of fellowship, oneness, awareness of traditions, family roots and heritage, a sense of freedom to speak, think and participate.*

**Celebrating** Here are some ideas and suggestions to stir up your own creativity. Choose what seems to fit your family, realizing that your ways of celebrating life will change as your family changes, but also that you may be starting traditions that will continue for generations.

Whatever pattern of religious celebration you develop, make it your own, enjoy it, and keep it flexible so that it can grow and change. Worshipping together can enrich your experience of life and deepen your relations with one another.

**Around the Dinner Table** If yours is one of those families that never seem able to sit down for a meal together, try to find at least one time during the week when this can happen. It may turn out to be a weekend breakfast instead of an evening meal. If, on the other hand, you regularly gather around the dinner table, you have more opportunities for the simple observances that can make the time together meaningful for all.

**Lighting a Chalice or a Candle** You can make your own chalice by placing a small votive candle in a shallow bowl. When you sit down together, take turns lighting the chalice and saying special words. You'll find suggestions in Chapter 5. Or simply say,

> *Today, I'm thankful for...*
> *This flame is to help us remember...*
> *Today, I'm thinking about...*
> *This day is important to me because...*

**Saying Grace**   Suggested table graces are also given in Chapter 5. Your family can collect lines of poetry or other readings that are meaningful for you; take turns saying grace in their own words; or hold hands around the table for a silent grace, passing around a hand-squeeze to say "Amen."

**Celebrating Milestones and Special Occasions**   Birthdays, of course! In addition to your usual practices, add a few minutes to reflect on the past year and share favorite memories of, by, or about the birthday person, ways in which s/he has grown, wishes and hopes for the coming year.

Other occasions warrant celebrations:  promotions, getting onto the team or into the chorus or school play, getting a driver's license, the baby's first words or first steps, or a "first time ever" or "first time this year" for just about anything significant to you.

Seasons of the year are natural points of celebration:  first days of spring, summer, autumn, and winter, and also those cross-quarter days halfway between equinox and solstice, such as Candlemas or Ground Hog Day, May Day, August 1 (Lammas to the ancients), Halloween or All Saints Day (a good Universalist holiday!).

**Birthdays of Famous UUs and Others**   Begin with the UUA calendar (available each year through the UUA Bookstore), and choose a "famous birthday" to celebrate for each month. Let various members of the family be responsible for decorations, food, and appropriate stories or readings or songs. If cake with candles is what makes it Happy Birthday time at your house, then do it for Thomas Jefferson and Clara Barton as well!

## Worshipping at Home

You can create your own worship services at home. Sunday morning is the traditional time, but you may find one that suits your family better. Weekly is the usual interval, but you might begin with a monthly service and move toward greater frequency.

**Create a Setting**   You may decide to do one of the following:
- Gather around a table with a chalice, candles, flowers, or special objects.
- Form a half circle of chairs around the fireplace, perhaps adding a special picture on the mantelpiece.
- Spread a bright-colored cloth on the floor, arranging bits of nature or art around your chalice in the center, and sitting around in a circle.
- Gather outdoors in a beautiful spot.

**Create a Pattern** Here is the format one CLF family uses for a Sunday morning service in their living room:

- Each member of the family lights a candle
- Opening words: a favorite poem or something appropriate from the newspaper, a magazine, or a book (also see Chapter 5)
- Recorded music
- Thoughts for the week: each person shares high points and low points of the past week, what they are looking forward to in the coming week, and anything they are worrying about
- Closing words or a song they sing together

They take turns doing the opening words and choosing the music. Sometimes they go on to do a session from a religious education curriculum borrowed from CLF.

**Here is Another Way to Create a Service Together:**

- Provide a box or paper bag into which you can drop ideas or themes for services as they occur to you: for example, P. T. Barnum's Birthday, or Harvest Moon, or Helping Others, or Making Our Home Ecologically Responsible, or Black History Month.
- After your family worship, but while you are still gathered in your worship space, someone reaches into the box or bag and pulls out a slip of paper with a theme.
- Decide among you who is to be responsible for 1) creating a visual focal point, 2) opening words, 3) a song, 4) a reading, and 5) a closing. Agree to present the service next time you gather.
- Do it!

You might also plan a service around religious questions that members of the family raise. Take some time to gather ideas and materials that focus on the question in different ways. Encourage other members of the family to say how they feel about the question or what their responses might be. The point, of course, is not so much to answer the question as to give it the attention and importance that it deserves and to keep those big questions coming.

# Chapter Two
# Child Namings and Dedications

The following two Unitarian Universalist child-naming and dedication services are distinctly different. You may use them exactly as presented, or "mix and match" elements in a service you create to meet the needs of a particular family and situation. *Remember that the bracketed [ ] portions in these services indicate where choices are to be made.*

Parents may wish to participate in planning the order and content of the service, perhaps adding favorite readings or poetry. A child naming and dedication is enriched by such personalization, and, if they are interested, the family should be invited to participate in a planning session scheduled well in advance of the service date.

If the parents come from differing faith traditions, the service may need to reflect this by being inclusive of both heritages. An obvious goal of any service is to make all in attendance feel welcomed, affirmed, and included.

Don't be surprised or disappointed, however, if a family declines the invitation to take an active part in the planning process. Many will prefer that you do all the preparation, and will gladly take part in whatever ways you indicate.

Once the elements of the service have been determined, a photocopy of the complete service should be made and arranged in the correct order. Write in the correct names and pronouns (and any other spoken parts unique to the service) as you will say them. This will ensure a smoothly-flowing service and will also help you avoid making unnecessary marks in this handbook.

Other logistics involved in the service will require your attention ahead of time. Plan how to set up the space where the service will occur to make it as attractive as possible. Perhaps you will want a table with a tablecloth, flowers, or candles. Think about where the participants will stand so that everyone in attendance will be able to see and enjoy the service, and inform all of the participants. If a flower and/or a certificate will be included, make sure you have them on hand.

Child namings and dedications are wonderful occasions, so enjoy your participation!

For additional naming and dedication service material appropriate in a Unitarian Universalist setting, see the book, *Great Occasions*, by Carl Seaburg, Beacon Press, Boston 1968. (*Available through UUA Bookstore, 25 Beacon Street, Boston, MA 02108*).

# A Child-Naming and Dedication Service

## Order of Service

Opening Words
Address to Those Gathered
    [Or] Responsive Reading
Address to Parents
Address to Godparents
    (*optional*)
Reading
Call to Children Attending
    (*optional*)
Naming and Dedication
Affirmation by Those
    in Attendance
Blessing of the Child
Benediction

## Checklist

Attractive container with
    room-temperature water
Printed copies of Responsive
    Reading and Affirmation
    for all attending
Choose: Address to People or
    Responsive Reading;
    whether to have a Call to
    Children.
Godparents' names
Flower

## Opening Words

The poet e. e. cummings reminds us:

"...we can never be born enough. we are human beings for whom birth is a supremely welcome mystery. the mystery of growing, the mystery which happens only and whenever we are faithful to ourselves. life for eternal us is now."

## Address to Those Gathered

*(Choose one of the following two sections.)*

The ceremony in which we now share is both ancient and timeless. In all parts of the earth, and from the earliest days of recorded history, parents have brought their children at an early age to a place of worship, sharing their joy and dedication with those of the wider community.

Traditionally, the element of water (*point to the water that is to be used in the ceremony*) has played a symbolic part in this ceremony, for all life has arisen from the waters, and it is through water that life is sustained as it flows forward like a river.

Traditionally also this is the time to recognize our children by name, for it is by name that each of us is acknowledged as a unique and separate person. The [flower/s] we shall present to [this child is/ these children are] also symbolic of the individuality we wish to affirm.

This is a public occasion, shared by parents, family, and friends, to mark the fact that we all have a responsibility for the care and nurturing of every child. It is our task to give them a world of peace and justice in which to grow. It is our task to share with them our ideals and hopes. It is our task to learn from them the zest and wonder of life, with which all children come into the world, and which we too often lose in later life.

**[Or]**

## Responsive Reading

*All:* **In welcoming a child, we celebrate the miracle of birth.**

*Leader:* This is a time for joy. We rejoice when a child is born into the care and concern, not only of parents, but also of our community.

*People:* **Every child born into the world needs the love and care of others. Each deserves to be held in loving arms and to be taught good ways of living.**

*Leader:* Each child has the right to know what it means to be human and what we must do to make life beautiful and good for ourselves, for each other, and for all the living beings who share this earth home with us.

*People:* **In welcoming a child, we celebrate our hopes for life.**


## Address to the Parents

[*First name of parent*                                          ] and
[*first name of parent*                                          ], to you
as parents let me say this: In presenting your child at this service, you invite all of us to share some of the joy and responsibility that is yours as parents. You seek our support in your dedication to the task of fostering, with love and guidance, the fullest unfolding of the personality of your child.

Your task may not always be an easy one. The time may come when you will be called upon to sacrifice ambitions, deny yourselves pleasure, or set aside your own dreams so that your child may tread more surely the onward path of life. But you accept this service to another life, knowing that your own lives will be fuller and richer in consequence.

Do you now promise that, to the best of your human abilities, you will help this child to an appreciation of truth and beauty, uprightness of character, and love? If so, say, "We do."

## Address to the Godparents
*Or special friends standing with the family*

[*First names of godparents* _____],
to you let me say this: An old Jewish proverb says, "In time of travail, go to the friend of your Father, go to the friend of your Mother." From this ancient wisdom comes the idea of godparents, or special people who dedicate themselves to watching out for the welfare of others' children. It is a noble and loving tradition to which you commit yourselves this day.

In our complex world, it is not possible for even the most loving and capable parents to raise a child alone. If our children are to become loving and independent adults, they need the wisdom, counsel, love, and support of many adult friends. You have been asked by the parents of this child to accept a special honor and responsibility.

Do you then, to the best of your abilities, intend to supplement the care and love of these parents, both in the day-to-day development of this child, and especially in the event of any extraordinary need? If so, say, "We do."

May this commitment and dedication enrich and ennoble your lives.

## Meditation
Let us join in meditation.

Spirit of Life, we are your children. Out of the infinite we have come to you and through you. We are the old, yet ever new, miracle of incarnation. Give us a chance to grow, within the warmth of your unfailing love, into souls sensitive to beauty, hearts open to love and hungry for the imperishable values of life. Do not shrink and wither us with fear, but quicken with faith the springs of courage within us.

Enter with us through the gates of wonder, into the wider perspectives of the morrow. Accept us as we grow into a fellowship of mutual respect and shared responsibility, that we in our turn may be worthy fathers and mothers of the coming generation.

*Source unknown*

## Reading for an Adopted Child *(when applicable)*

We did not plant you...

True.

But when the season is done

    when the alternate prayers for sun and rain are counted

When the pain of weeding and the pride of watching are through

Then will we hold you high,

    a shining sheaf above the thousand seed grown wild.

Not by our planting

    but, by heaven, our harvest,

Our child.

*Source unknown*

## Naming and Dedication

*The leader can either hold the infant—placing the service on the table, or have the pages held by someone so it can be read—or have the parents or god-parents continue to hold the infant.*

[*Parents' first names*                                  ],

by what name is this child known? *(Parents give complete name of child; leader will have written name in advance in space below.)*

*(Leader dips fingers in water and touches child's forehead.)*

[*Leader repeats complete name*                        ],

I touch your young brow with water from old nature's infinite sky, water that touches every shore and nourishes every race of people. In so doing I dedicate your life and thought to the good of all humankind and to your own true growing.

I also give you this flower, unique in all its natural beauty, separate and distinct from all other flowers found in creation, to express symbolically our hope that all your life long you will unfold and blossom just as you must, in all of your own unique and natural beauty.

(*Leader then lays a hand on the child's forehead and says:*) May the blessings of an understanding heart, strength and integrity of purpose, and love received and given, be yours and remain with you as you go forward into ever fuller life. Amen.

## Affirmation by Those in Attendance

Would you all please rise and join with me in saying the affirmation printed before you:

**As we contemplate the miracle of birth, as we renew in our hearts a sense of wonder and joy, may we be stirred to a fresh awareness of the sacredness of life and of the divine promise of childhood. May we so live that our children may acquire our best virtues and leave behind our worst failings. May we pass on the light of courage and compassion and the questing spirit, and may that light burn more brightly in this child than it has in us.**

## Call to Children in Attendance (*optional*)

I invite the children present to come forward now. (*Children come forward.*) You are closest to this child in age and will be working and playing and growing in the same world together. It is good that at this time [s/he] should be surrounded by you and your good wishes. There is another reason for you to be here. In dedicating this child, we all rejoice and give thanks for the presence of all children in our lives. And while the words we say and the promises we make for this child are meant especially for [him/her], they are also meant for you.

## Charge to the Children (*optional*)

Today we welcome [*name of child*              ].
As [s/he] grows, [s/he] will look up to you older children. Will you be a friend to [her/him]? Will you speak to [her/him] with kindness and treat [her/him] with fairness? Will you show [her/him] the best that is in you and help [her/him] to discover the best that is in [her/him]? If you will, please answer, "Yes." (*Children may return to their seats.*)

## Blessing of the Child

And we bless you now, [*name of child*                    ],
with this ancient Irish blessing:

May the blessing of the light be with you always, light without and light within. May the sun shine upon you and warm your heart until it glows like a great fire so that others may feel the warmth of it. And may the light of your eyes shine like two candle lights in a window at night, bidding the wanderer to come in out of the dark and the cold. And may the blessings of the rain be upon you, the sweet and tender rain; may it fall upon your spirit as when flowers spring up and fragrance fills the air. And may the blessings of the great rain wash you clean and fair, and may the storms always leave you stronger and more beautiful. And when the rains are over, may there be clear pools of water, made beautiful by the radiance of your light, as when a star shines, beautiful in the night, pointing the way for all of us.

## Benediction

We have dedicated [*name of child*                    ].
May we also dedicate ourselves this day. May this occasion work its miracle in our hearts, that we may mold our lives more and more in accordance with the beauty, truth, goodness, and love we wish for the life of [*name of child*                    ].

18

# A Short Service of Child Recognition

*This service includes the presentation of a dedication certificate and a flower, both of which need to be obtained before the service is conducted. A UU dedication certificate may be obtained by writing to the UUA Bookstore, 25 Beacon Street, Boston, MA 02108.*

**Order of Service**
Opening Words
Charge to Parents
Naming
Charge to Community
Presentation of Certificate
    and Flower
Benediction

**Checklist**
Certificate, completed in
    advance
Flower

## Opening Words

In the ancient tradition of all human society, we have come together to welcome and to recognize among us the great and persistent mystery of ongoing human life and to recognize the need for a family of mutual support.

In our Western religious tradition we hear Moses declaring, "See, I have set before thee this day, life and good, and death and evil; therefore, choose life, that both thou and thy seed may live." And Jesus said, "Suffer the little children to come unto me, and forbid them not."

From the scriptures of the East we read, "In their teachings, superior parents guide their children but do not pull them along; they urge them to go forward and do not suppress them; they open the way but do not take them to the place."

And the poet Gibran wrote, "Your children are not your children. They are the sons and daughters of Life's longing for itself. You may give them your love but not your thoughts. You may house their bodies but not their souls, for their souls dwell in the house of tomorrow, which you cannot visit, not even in your dreams. And though they are with you they belong not to you."

## Charge to Parents

Friends, you bring your child to be recognized as a testimony to the universal mystery of ongoing human life. Will you endeavor to instruct [her/him] that [s/he] may be taught human love by feeling human love, taught justice by the laws that rule [her/his] days; taught wisdom by the way in which [s/he] lives, taught to love all people and serve them fair by seeing from [her/his] birth other children served with the same righteous, all-embracing care? If so, answer, "We will."

## Naming

*(If recognizing more than one child, name them and confirm their names one at a time. Leader should write name/s in spaces below, in advance.)*

What name have you given this child?

*(Parents answer:)* [*child's name* ]

In the name of love and life, I confirm to you the name of [*child's name* ].

## Charge to the Wider Community

Our children are not put into the hands of parents alone. They are brought at birth into a vast and infinite school. The universe is charged with the office of their education. Nature, society, and experience are volumes opened everywhere and perpetually before their eyes. They take lessons from every object within the sphere of their senses and their activity, from the sun and stars, from the flowers of spring and the fruits of autumn, from every associate, from every smiling and frowning countenance, from their friend-ships and dislikes, from the varieties of human character, and from the consequences of their actions.

*William Ellery Channing*

We perform this ceremony to declare that all of us, as parents and as members of society, are responsible for the care and nurture of all children. It is our task to give them a world of peace and justice in which to grow. It is our task to give them our ideals and our hopes.

By dedicating [*name of child/ren* ]
here today, these parents acknowledge that children are more than private possessions, but are new beings for whom we all have a responsibility, and therefore all welcome to the community.

## Presentation of Certificate and Flower
*(Present the certificate to the parents.)*
When [s/he] has come to years of understanding, we hope that you
will give [her/him] this certificate, that [s/he] may know how great
is the endowment of love and concern with which [s/he] started life.

*(Present the flower to the parents.)*
As this flower unfolds in natural beauty, so may [her/his] life unfold,
and may this flower also serve to remind you of the commitments
that you have made this day.


## Benediction
We have dedicated this child,
And in so doing, we give thanks for the gift of life.
With each child we renew in our hearts our sense of wonder and joy.
We commit ourselves to this child and to all children, to this world
and to its betterment.    Amen.

## Chapter Three
# Wedding Services

The following are distinctly different Unitarian Universalist wedding services. You may use them exactly as presented, or combine elements to create a service that meets the needs of each particular couple and situation. *Remember that a bracketed [ ] portion in the service indicates where choices are to be made.*

One of the first things that must be done in preparing for a marriage service is to make sure that you conform to all legal requirements. Every state and province has laws concerning who may and may not officiate at weddings, how a wedding license is obtained, and other requirements. If you reside in a place where only clergy and justices are allowed to certify a marriage, you, as a UU lay leader, can probably conduct a legal wedding by having an official person on hand to sign the license. **Before you conduct a wedding, you must check with the local authorities to ensure that you do not violate any laws!**

Many wedding couples wish to participate in planning the order, content, and style of the service, perhaps writing their own vows and adding favorite poetry and readings. In these cases, a planning meeting should be arranged well in advance of the wedding date to allow for adequate preparation time.

Weddings are enriched by such personalization and participation, but don't be surprised or disappointed if a couple declines your invitation to take an active role in the planning of the service. Some will prefer that you do all or most of the preparation; however, most couples are happy to be given choices about certain elements and readings, and even this minimal involvement should be encouraged.

If the two individuals to be married come from differing faith traditions, the service may need to reflect this by including elements and readings from both heritages. Obviously, any religious service should strive to make everyone in attendance feel welcome and included.

Once the wedding service order and elements have been determined, a photocopy of the complete service should be made and arranged in the correct order. Write in the correct names and pronouns (and any other spoken parts unique to the service) as you will say them. This will ensure a smoothly-flowing service and also help you avoid making unnecessary marks in this handbook.

Other service logistics will require your attention ahead of time. You need to determine how the space will be arranged, where the guests will stand or sit, where the participants in the service will stand, and on which cues participants will enter and exit. If any objects are included in the service (wine, chalice, flowers) you will need to plan where to place them conveniently and attractively.

**Services of Holy Union for Same-Gender Couples:** In 1984, the delegates to the General Assembly of the Unitarian Universalist Association overwhelmingly passed a resolution affirming gay and lesbian services of union and encouraging all ministers and congregations to support "...this important aspect of our movement's ministry to the gay and lesbian community."

Because no North American state or province yet legally recognizes same-gender unions, a service celebrating such a union is a purely religious ceremony. When we conduct a same-gender union service, we are affirming our support as Unitarian Universalists for gay and lesbian couples who wish to commit their lives to each other and live together in stable partnerships.

The structure and content of such a service can be very similar to a typical heterosexual wedding, for what is being affirmed is the universal value of love and commitment. The service should acknowledge (and even celebrate) the struggle that lies ahead for any same-gender couple.

Weddings and Holy Unions are wonderful and affirming occasions, so enjoy your participation!

For additional wedding materials appropriate in a UU setting, see *Great Occasions*, by Carl Seaburg, Beacon Press, Boston, 1968. This book can be purchased through the UUA Bookstore at 25 Beacon St., Boston, MA 02108. The UUA's Office of Lesbian and Gay Concerns, 25 Beacon St., Boston MA, 02108, has a complete *Planning Guide for Services of Holy Union*.

# Wedding Service I

## Order Of Service
Opening Words
Wedding Address
Blessings
Reading
Introduction to the Vows
Vows
Exchange of Ring/s
Reading
Pronouncement
Benediction

## Checklist
Parents' names (if Blessing used)
Bride's and groom's names as they wish them to be used in the service
Choose option to use:
for vows
for ring exchange
for benediction

## Opening Words
If life has meaning to us at all, it possesses it because of love. It is that which enshrines and ennobles our human experience. It is the basis for the peace of family and the peace of the peoples of the earth. The greatest gift bestowed upon humans is the gift not of demanding but of giving love between two persons.

*Source unknown*

## Wedding Address
In marriage, two persons turn to each other in search of a greater fulfillment than either can achieve alone. Marriage is a going forth, a bold step into the future; it is risking what we are for the sake of what we yet can be. Only in giving oneself and sharing with another can the mysterious process of growth take place. Only in loyalty and devotion bestowed upon another can that which is eternal in life emerge and be known. Two among us, who have stood apart, come now, in our presence, to declare their love and to be united in marriage.

Love is a living thing, waiting within each one of us for an awakening touch. In this ceremony, we will celebrate love come to life. May this love grow sure and straight and strong. We rejoice in its presence among us.

*Source unknown*

24

## Blessings

*(When not appropriate or comfortable, parents' blessing can be omitted. It can be used even though one or more of the parents is missing.)*

From time immemorial, weddings such as this one have been public occasions where family and friends gather to express the joy and approval that they feel for the new union.

Let me therefore ask you parents this:
Do you, [*first names of groom's parents*                    ],
and you, [*first names of bride's parents*                    ],
who have raised and nurtured these two, give your blessings now to them as they enter into this new relationship, and do you aspire in the days and years ahead to give them your deepest love, understanding, and support during both good times and bad? If so, say, "We do."

And let me ask the rest of you gathered here today: Do you who know and care for [*couple's first names*                    ] give them your blessings now as they enter into this new relationship, and do you aspire in the days and years ahead to give them your deepest love, understanding, and support during both good times and bad? If so, say, "We do."

*Scott W. Alexander*

## Reading

Walt Whitman wrote:

"Listen! I will be honest with you. I do not offer the old smooth prizes, but offer rough new prizes. These are the days that must happen to you. You shall not heap up what is called riches, you shall scatter with lavish hand all that you earn or achieve. However sweet these laid-up stores, however convenient this dwelling, we cannot remain here. However shelter'd this port and however calm these waters, we must not anchor here. However welcome the hospitality that surrounds us, we are permitted to receive it but a little while. Come, I give you my hand! I give you my love more precious than money. I give you myself before preaching or law. Will you give me yourself? Will you come travel with me? Shall we stick by each other as long as we live?"

## Introduction to the Vows

[*First names of bride and groom*                    ],
it is a great joy and pleasure for me to be standing here with you on
this momentous day, sharing in your marriage ceremony, and
witnessing to the life-long commitment you are making to one
another this day.

I must remind you that the vows you are about to say to one another
belong entirely to you. The words I speak have no magical powers,
and nothing that I can say or do on this day can ultimately make
your marriage endure with beauty, fidelity, and joy. Only you, by the
integrity and diligence of your love, can make these vows last.

So it is not to lofty words, or institutions even, that we appeal at this
hour of commitment; but rather to the resources which you two can
draw from deep within yourselves...the deep well of human need, the
need to live united and loving and complete before a broken and
imperfect world. So will you now please join a hand each to each,
and repeat your vows after me?

*Scott W. Alexander*

*(Couple joins right hands.)*

## Vows

*(Speak the wedding vows to each person to repeat, one line at a time.)*

In reaffirming the relationship we have been building together,
I [                    ] take you [                    ]
to be no other than yourself.
Loving what I know of you,
trusting what I don't yet know,
with respect for your integrity
and faith in your abiding love for me,
through all our years,
and in all that life shall bring us,
I accept you as my [wife/husband].
*(Repeat vow for second person.)*

**[Or]**

I take you [                    ] to be my [wife/husband],
loving you now and always.
I will love you when we are together and when we are apart,
when life is peaceful and when it is in disorder,
when I am proud of you and when I am disappointed in you.
I will honor your goals and dreams
and help you to fulfill them.

From my heart I will seek to be open and honest with you.
I say these things believing that God is in the midst of them all.
*[Alternative last sentence:* I say these things to you with the whole of
my being.] *(Repeat vow for second person.)*

**[Or]**

In reaffirming the relationship we have been building together,
I [_____] now take you [_____] in marriage.
Together in love,
to work and to share,
to grow and understand,
to discover a deeper, fuller life. *(Repeat vow for second person.)*

**[Or]**

In reaffirming the relationship we have been building together,
I take you to be my [wife/husband],
to be the [mother/father] of my children,
to be the companion of my days.
We shall bear together
whatever of sorrow and adversity life may lay upon us.
We shall share together
whatever of joy and fulfillment
life may hold in store. *(Repeat vow for second person.)*

## Exchange Of Ring/s

Love freely given has no giver and no receiver. You are each the
giver and each the receiver. [_____] and
[_____], by the use of [this/ these ring/s] you
express, in visible form, the unbroken circle of your love, so that
wherever you go, you may always return to your shared life
together. May [this/ these ring/s] always call to mind the freedom
and power of this love.

[_____], as you place this ring on
[_____]'s finger, please repeat after me:

"I give you this ring...to wear upon your hand...as a symbol of our
commitment and love."

*(If two rings are exchanged, repeat for second person.)*

**[Or]**

Black Elk, an Oglala Sioux, has written:

"Everything the Power of the World does is done in a circle. The sky is round, and I have heard that the earth is round like a ball and so are the stars. The wind in its greatest power whirls. Birds make their nests in circles, for theirs is the same religion as ours. The sun comes forth and goes down again in a circle. Even the seasons form a great circle in their changing, and always come back again to where they were. The life of a man or a woman is a circle from childhood to childhood, and so it is in everything where power moves."

*Used with permission*

[_____], as you place this ring on
[_____]'s finger, please repeat after me:

"I give you this ring ... to wear upon your hand ... as a symbol of our commitment and love."

*(If two rings are exchanged, repeat for second person.)*

## Reading
Anne Morrow Lindberg has written:

"When you love someone, you do not love them all the time, in exactly the same way, from moment to moment. It is an impossibility, it is even a lie to pretend to. And yet this is exactly what most of us demand. We have so little faith in the ebb and flow of life, of love, of relationships. We leap at the flow of the tide and resist in terror its ebb. We are afraid it will never return. We insist on permanency, on duration, on continuity; when the only continuity possible in life, as in love, is in growth, in fluidity, in freedom, in the sense that the dancers are free, barely touching as they pass, but partners in the same pattern.

"The only real security is not in owning or possessing, not in demanding or expecting, not in hoping even. Security in a relationship lies neither in looking back to what it was in nostalgia, nor forward to what it might be in dread or anticipation, but living in the present relationship and accepting it as it is now. For relationships too must be like islands. One must accept them for what they are here and now, within their limits. Islands, surrounded and interrupted by the sea, and continually visited and abandoned by the tides. One must accept the security of the winged life, of the ebb and flow, of intermittency."

## Pronouncement

[_____] and [_____],
you have told me, and all of your friends and family members who
have gathered here to share this moment of joy with you, that you
deeply love one another, and wish to live together now seeking an
ever-richer, ever-deeper relationship. You have formed your own
union—in friendship, in respect for one another, and in love—and it
is therefore now my joyful task to acknowledge you as husband and
wife.

*(Couple may kiss.)*

## Benediction

And now, may that glory which rests on all who love, rest upon you,
and bless you and keep you, and fill you with happiness and a
gracious spirit. And, despite all changes of time and fortune, may all
that is noble and lovely and true abound in your hearts, and abide
with you, and give you strength in all your days together.

**[Or]**

[_____] and [_____],
believe in what is yours, believe in who you are, believe in the
richness and the power of what lies in the depths you share. And go
now in great happiness assured that all our hearts go with you.

# Wedding Service II

*This service should be conducted with the couple facing a small table or a fireplace. On the table or fireplace mantel, two goblets of wine should be placed attractively, along with an arrangement of flowers, if desired. In one goblet there should be a small amount of sweet wine and in the other, bitter or dry wine.*

| Order of Service | Checklist |
|---|---|
| Opening Words | Choose options in service |
| Wine Ceremony | Set up table |
| Exchange of Vows | Prepare goblets with wine |
| Exchange of Rings | Bride's and groom's names as |
| Wedding Prayer | they wish them to be used |
| Pronouncement | |
| Benediction | |

## Opening Words

Dear Friends: [We have come together/ We are gathered here in the presence of God and in the presence of this company] to join these two in marriage, which is an institution made creative by the loving care of men and women of all time.

It is, therefore, not to be entered into lightly or unadvisedly, but reverently, intelligently, soberly. Into this closest of relationships you two come to be joined by a ceremony which, to be true, must be but a symbol of something inner and real—a sacred union of hearts and lives—which religion may bless and the state make legal, but which neither can create or annul. You two, only, may do that.

[*Groom's first name*                                        ], will you have
[*bride's first name*                                        ] to be your
wife? Will you love her, respect her, comfort and keep her? Will you share with her in sickness and in health, in sorrow and in joy, [so long as you both shall live/ from this day forward]?

(*Groom answers*) I will.

[*Bride's first name*                                        ], will you have
[*groom's first name*                                        ] to be your
husband? Will you love him, respect him, comfort and keep him? Will you share with him in sickness and in health, in sorrow and in joy, [so long as you both shall live/ from this day forward]?

(*Bride answers*) I will.

*(Optional)*
[Who presents this bride in marriage/ Who pledges the good will of the families of this couple]?

*(Parents answer as appropriate:)* [I/We] do.

## Wine Ceremony

You were born together, and together you shall be....
But let there be spaces in your togetherness,
And let the winds of the heavens dance between you.
Love one another, but make not a bond of love:...
Sing and dance together and be joyous, but let each one of you be
        alone,
Even as the strings of a lute are alone though they quiver with the
        same music.
Give your hearts, but not into each other's keeping....
And stand together yet not too near together:
For the pillars of the temple stand apart,
And the oak tree and the cypress grow not in each other's shadow.

*Kahlil Gibran*
*Used with permission*

It is the goal of marriage to achieve a blending of hearts and lives—but let there be spaces in your new life together, so that each may encourage and nurture the individual growth of the other. Even so, your separate lives will become one life; your separate homes, one home; your separate fortunes, one fortune.

Over the horizon of the future, there come toward you even now hours of brightness and hours of shadow, for such is the nature of life.

*(Pick up the goblet of sweet wine.)*

Life has, indeed, many bright and happy experiences, of which this sweet wine is a token. As you drink of it together, may it serve as a symbol of the joy that comes with loving and sharing, and may your happiness be tempered with gratitude and modesty and a bountiful sympathy for those who are less fortunate than you.

*(Pass goblet to bride, who drinks and passes it to groom, who drinks and passes it back to you. Return goblet to table and pick up goblet of bitter wine.)*

But when hardship and sorrow and disappointment come, of which this bitter wine is a token, may you care enough to help one another with courage and compassion, neither one blaming the other for folly or failure, or regretting the obligation of marriage to share and bear together the chances and changes of a life deeply lived.

*(Goblet is passed as above.)*

## Exchange of Vows

*(Read the vows in phrases of appropriate length.)*

Now, join your right hands and repeat after me:

"I, [*groom's first name*                        ], take you,
[*bride's first name*                        ], to be my wife,
to have and to hold, for better, for worse, for richer, for poorer, in sickness and in health, to love, cherish, and respect, [from this day forward/ so long as we both shall live]."

"I, [*bride's first name*                        ], take you,
[*groom's first name*                        ], to be my
husband, to have and to hold, for better, for worse, for richer, for poorer, in sickness and in health, to love, cherish, and respect, [from this day forward/ so long as we both shall live]."

## Exchange Of Ring/s

What [symbol/s] do you have of these vows that you take?

*(Ring/s are placed in leader's hand.)*

[These rings are/ This ring is] of gold; so may your love for each other be the most precious possession of your lives. A ring constitutes a circle; may it symbolize the never-ending loyalty and honor that shall encompass and bind your new relationship.

Take this ring, [*groom's name*             ], and place it upon the third finger of [*bride's name*          ]'s left hand, saying these words: "With the giving of this ring, I thee wed."

[*Bride's name*                    ], will you say, "With the receiving of this ring, I thee wed."

*(If there is a second ring, continue:)* Take this one, [*bride's name* _____], and place it upon the third finger of [*groom's name* _____]'s left hand, saying these words: "With the giving of this ring, I thee wed."

[*Groom's name* _____], will you say, "With the receiving of this ring, I thee wed."

## Wedding Prayer

Let us pray: [Eternal Spirit/ Creative Source of life/ Dear God], in the midst of which we live and move and have our being: in thy name are we met together, to witness and to bless the union of these two lives. May it be in their hearts and in their powers, faithfully to consummate and keep the pledges of this day. May they be a blessing and comfort, each to the other, sharers of each other's sorrows, helpers of each other in all the chances and changes of the world. May they grow in understanding and love, and may faithfulness to the good of each become the unfailing virtue of them both. Amen.

## Pronouncement

Whom love hath joined together let no one break asunder. For as much as you two have consented to live together in marriage and have pledged yourselves to each other, and have declared the same by giving and receiving [(a) ring/s] and by joining hands, I, therefore, in the name of high religion, do pronounce you husband and wife.

*(Couple may kiss.)*

Think not that you have finished anything here today. This service is but the mark of a beginning. Today before all the world you have formally lighted the lamp of love. Keep it warm and bright with mutual concern. Replenish the source of its light with daily care, with gentleness and respect. Take it with you into all the highways and byways of life. Try it. But let it not burn dry with your indifference or flicker and grow dim through your carelessness. Care for it. Rejoice in it. Make it a light truly creative in your lives and in the larger life of which all of us are a part.

## Benediction
*(Use either or both.)*

And, now, as you go out from this place together, and in love, may the blessings of those around you [*optional:* and the benediction of the Most High] attend you and keep you—together always, in understanding, tenderness, and love.   Amen.

**[And/or]**

Let us conclude this ceremony with a Native American blessing:

May you feel no rain, for each of you will be shelter to the other.

May you feel no cold, for each of you will be warmth to the other.

May there be no loneliness for you.

Now you are two bodies, but there is one life before you.

Go now to your dwelling-place, to enter into the days of your togetherness.

And may your days be good, and long upon the earth.

*Adapted from the Apache by Kenneth Patton*

# Holy Union Service Components

What follows is a sample order of service and several components that could be included in a service of union for same-gender couples. This is not a complete service; please refer to the other two wedding services in this chapter for appropriate readings and components.

| Order of Service | Checklist |
| --- | --- |
| Opening Words/Poem | (Compile your own checklist: |
| **Address** | e.g., rings, flowers) |
| Reading/Poem | |
| Exchange of Vows | |
| Exchange of Rings | |
| Reading/Poem | |
| **Pronouncement** | |
| Benediction | |

## Address

It is written that the greatest of all things—the most wonderful experience in the world—is love.

[*Couple's names*_____],
into your lives has entered a deep and nurturing love, and you have asked [this Unitarian Universalist congregation/me as a Unitarian Universalist religious leader] to help you celebrate and affirm that love.

We would call your love partnership a "Holy Union," for wherever there is love, [God/that which is holy] abides there also. For as long as men and women have walked on the earth, there have been some human beings who have shared their deepest expression of love with a person of the same gender. Our faith tradition, Unitarian Universalism, has grown to recognize the validity and beauty of that special way of loving, and strives with others to overcome the prejudice and fear about it in our society. It is our hope that one day all true love partnerships may be legally recognized and fully affirmed.

[*Couple's names*_____],
you have honored us by inviting us to witness your commitment to each other in Holy Union. May your love grow sure and strong and true in the days and years of your shared life together.

## Pronouncement
*(Choose one of the following two options)*

[*Couple's names*                                                  ], for as
much as you have committed yourselves to one another—and, in
token of this bond, have spoken your vows [*optional:* and exchanged
rings]—by the authority vested in me as a [minister/leader] of this
Unitarian Universalist congregation, I recognize you as united in
Holy Union. You may [kiss/embrace].

*Scott W. Alexander*

**[Or]**

By the authority of Life itself,

By the life that fills and surrounds us

And that reaches toward another for fulfillment

And to share deeply,

By the day given to us to live,

And by the cycle of seasons through which our lives must pass in
    change,

By the love of friends that honors and supports this loving
    relationship, and

By the hurts and pain through which your lives have passed alone,

By the long and sometimes lonely struggle of gay and lesbian
    persons for the freedom to love,

And by the delight and hope you have found in each other,

I say that you are united in a covenant, and I call your union holy.

Let all respect the threshold of your home.

I congratulate you.

Let us go forth energized by the grace of this love.

*F. Jay Deacon*

# Chapter Four
# Memorial Services

What follows are two simple and complete memorial services and a committal service, any of which could be conducted without the involvement of clergy. While the services are reasonably straightforward, you will notice that there are quite a few choices and decisions to be made before the service. [*Remember that the bracketed [ ] portions in the service indicate where choices are to be made.*]

A memorial service requires substantial care and sensitivity to plan and conduct. As long as you remember that the purpose of the service is to minister to the loved ones, you can create a meaningful and effective service.

The element that requires the most attention is the Personal Reflections/Eulogy, which should be prepared carefully. Although a service can be planned without this personal element, generally a service is much more effective if such an individualized component is included.

Many Unitarian Universalist memorial services are greatly enriched when the service leader encourages congregational participation in this "remembering" section of the service, allowing a relaxed and quiet time for individuals to speak of memories and feelings about the deceased. If you did not know the person, it might be possible to get the family or friends of the deceased to write a remembrance/eulogy for you, based on their intimate knowledge. Or you might meet with them a day or two before the service and then write a eulogy based on what you learn, possibly including key phrases or quotations from the family and friends. In the Unitarian Universalist tradition, remarks in this section of the service are usually focused upon the legacy which the deceased person has left as an enduring presence in the lives of those who remain, though other expressions of thought and feeling may be appropriate. Speakers should address the positive life contributions of the one being remembered, at whatever length and style seems to fit the occasion. Humor and honesty often make this section of the service particularly authentic and rewarding.

Because the death of an individual is usually a highly emotional event, those conducting the memorial service are wise to involve loved ones in the planning and preparation of the service and related events such as receptions or other gatherings. Inclusion of those who were close to the deceased is crucial to the success and meaningfulness of the service.

Those who knew and loved the deceased individual can be asked to contribute readings, music, flowers, or a "remembrance object" for the worship space, or a personal remembrance/eulogy to be read by that person or someone else. Decisions need to be made about the time and place for the service, as well as its basic mood, composition, length, and theological tone.

All of this requires careful planning, so make sure you set aside enough time to work with the family and loved ones to achieve a comfortable consensus. Loved ones often need to talk repeatedly about the death event and the deceased person, and the process of creating memorial service events may be as healing and helpful as the service itself.

Because of the spiritual diversity found among us, loved ones and family members do not always agree on such matters in their vulnerability and pain. The service leader/s should do everything possible to ensure that everyone's needs and perspectives get addressed and affirmed. Such intentional inclusiveness may mean that the service will have several distinct "spiritual voices," which reflects the open and inclusive spirit of our Unitarian Universalist heritage.

Once you have determined the memorial service order and elements, you should make a photocopy of the complete service and arrange it in the correct order. Write in the correct names and pronouns and any other spoken parts unique to the service. This will ensure a smooth-flowing service and also help you avoid making unnecessary marks in this handbook.

## Family Decisions
Families have many non-service-related decisions to make when someone dies—what to say in the obituary, whether to bury the body or cremate it, what to do about organ donations, and so on. The following list of resources may be helpful in such instances.

## Books
Morgan, Ernest, *Dealing Creatively with Death.* Burnsville, NC: Celo Press, 1988. A manual of death education and simple burial.

Grollman, Earl A. (ed.), *Concerning Death: A Practical Guide for the Living.* Boston: Beacon Press, 1974. Chapters on Protestant, Catholic, and Jewish theology and rituals of death and afterlife; children and death; final arrangements; bereavement; suicide; and condolence calls and letters.

Grollman, Earl A., *Talking about Death: A Dialogue Between Parent and Child.* Boston: Beacon Press, 1971. Models a direct and gentle way of discussing a death in the family, exploring the child's feelings, and reassuring him or her.

Seaburg, Carl, *Great Occasions*. Boston: Beacon Press, 1968. A collection of readings and poetry.

**Sources of Information**

*National Hospice Organization*. 1901 N. Fort Myer Drive, Suite 402, Arlington, VA 22209, (703) 243-5900. NHO is the national coordinating body for hospice organizations.

*Memorial Society Association of Canada*, Box 96, Station A, Weston, Ontario M9N 3M6.

*Continental Association of Funeral and Memorial Societies* (CAFMS), 2001 S Street, N.W., Suite 630, Washington, DC 20009, (202) 462-8888.

*Eye Bank Association of America*. 1511 K Street, N.W., Suite 830, Washington, DC 20005-1401, (202) 628-4280. Develops standards, professional training, and computer coordination, and monitors government activity and the media.

*Organ Donors Canada*. 5326 Ada Boulevard, Edmonton, Alberta T5W 4N7, (403) 474-9363. Founded in 1974, this is a nonprofit lay organization devoted to increasing public awareness of the need for organ and tissue donation.

*United Network for Organ Sharing (UNOS)*. P.O. Box 28010, Richmond, VA 23228, (804) 289-5380. Founded in 1984, a nationwide, computerized network for matching transplant donations and recipients.

## Committal Services

Often (either in addition to a memorial service or funeral, or in its place) there is a request for a committal service. In cases where the body of the deceased is being buried, such a service is conducted at graveside just before interment. In cases where the body has been cremated, the service takes place where the ashes are to be scattered or buried. (Note: each state or province has its own laws about disposition of the remains; you must check to make sure you are not participating in an illegal activity.)

Committal services are usually brief, including a reading or two, a prayer, words of committal, and possibly a benediction. Materials included in the sample memorial service could be used. In cases where the commital is the only service being held, the service could be longer, with family and friends invited to share memories, thoughts, and readings or prayers before the words of committal and disposition of the remains. It usually helps to let those attending know in advance that there will be an opportunity for such sharing. Individuals can be encouraged to write down what they want to say, or at least to mentally organize their remarks ahead of time.

# A Memorial Service

## Order of Service
Opening Words
Chalice/Candle Lighting
Address
Readings
Personal Reflections/Eulogy
Readings *(optional)*
Summation
Benediction

## Checklist
Choose opening words
Candle or chalice in place
Matches or lighter on hand
Eulogy prepared
Speakers prepared
Plans noted for disposition of
body

## Opening Words
*(Choose one of the following two options.)*

For everything there is a season,
     and a time for every matter under heaven:
A time to be born and a time to die;
A time to plant and a time to pluck up what is planted;
A time to kill and a time to heal;
A time to break down and a time to build up;
A time to weep and a time to laugh;
A time to mourn and a time to dance;
A time to cast away stones and a time to gather stones together;
A time to embrace and a time to refrain from embracing;
A time to seek and a time to lose;
A time to keep and a time to cast away;
A time to rend and a time to sew;
A time to keep silence and a time to speak;
A time to love and a time to hate;
A time for war and a time for peace.
For everything there is a season,
     and a time for every matter under heaven.
*Ecclesiastes, adapted*

## [Or]

Let us be honest with death. Let us not pretend that it is less than it is. It is separation. It is sorrow. It is grief. But let us neither pretend that death is more than it is. It is not annihilation. As long as memory endures, [her/his] influence will be felt. It is not an end to love—humanity's need for love from each of us is boundless. It is not an end to joy and laughter—nothing would less honor a [gentle/ kind/vibrant/ *other appropriate adjectives that describe the deceased could be substituted* ] soul than to make our lives drab in counterfeit respect. Let us be honest with death, for in that honesty we will understand [her/him] better and ourselves more deeply.

*Source unknown*

## Chalice or Candle Lighting
*Have a chalice or candle placed attractively so as to make it a focal point for the service.*

No one entering this world can ever escape sadness. Each in turn must bear burdens, though he or she be rich or poor, and in turn bid loved ones farewell as they set out upon life's ventures. Each one must suffer that sad farewell when loved ones embark on the last voyage, and each in turn must take that final journey. But for those who make this life a pledge to the spirit, there comes the assurance of a victory that shall redeem life's pain. (*Light candle or chalice.*) Though our spirit be but the feeble glow of a single flame, for the one who keeps it burning bravely to the end, death is not defeat. We light our [candle/chalice] today to honor the life and living of [*name of deceased*                            ].

*Robert Terry Weston (adapted)*

## Address
We have gathered here [*describe setting, e.g., in this place of human aspiration and hope/ in this beautiful setting/*

                                                                          ]
to acknowledge the death of [*name of deceased*                    ],
whom we have known and loved. When someone we have cared for dies, [*describe situation of death, e.g., especially as in this case after a long and fulfilling life/ especially as in this case when death has come tragically/ prematurely/*

                                                                          ],
family and friends gather with sorrow in their hearts. At times when we must face death and loss, we need one another's company for understanding and support. Just to be together, to look into one another's faces, takes away some of our loneliness and draws our hearts together in the healing which we can offer one another. At such times, the various faiths that sustain us separately come together in a harmony that acts across all creeds and assures us of the permanence of human goodness and hope.

So we have gathered here today in grief and sorrow, but we have also gathered to celebrate a life. We have come together to give thanks that we knew this [*appropriate adjective, e.g., gentle/ caring/ fine/ decent/*                              ] person, to express our gratitude for the days and years we were able to share with [her/him]. We are here to remember and memorialize a [*describe the outstanding personal qualities of the deceased with several adjectives, e.g.,* good/ gentle/ caring/ loyal/

]

life. By remembering the best of this person, by recalling some of [her/his] finest qualities, by honoring the principles, values, and dreams which guided [her/his] life, some of [*name of deceased*

]'s enduring nobility flows into us, that we ourselves might be more noble in the days ahead.

We are here for all these things. But our first spiritual task is to face, full and unafraid, the reality of this death, and the grief and loss we feel.

*Scott W. Alexander*

## Readings
*(Any or all of the following readings can be used.)*

A. Powell Davies wrote:

"When sorrow comes, let us accept it simply, as a part of life. Let the heart be open to pain; let it be stretched by it. All the evidence we have says that this is the better way. An open heart never grows bitter. Or if it does, it cannot remain so. In the desolate hour, there is an outcry, a clenching of the hands upon emptiness, a burning pain of bereavement, a weary ache of loss. But anguish, like ecstasy, is not forever. There comes a gentleness, a returning quietness, a restoring stillness. This, too, is a door to life. Here, also, is a deepening of meaning—and it can lead to dedication, a going forward to the triumph of the soul, the conquering of the wilderness. In the process will come a deepening inward knowledge that, in the final reckoning, all is well."

**[And/or]**

Frank Carleton Doan has written:

"This death of the body, is it not in the natural order of things in the
physical universe? Behold the flowers of the field. They bloom for a
brief season and then wither away. The birds of the air, they ascend
for their last flight, then descend to fold their wings and find peace
in their nest, even the peace of death. So, too, it is with the beasts of
the forest. When their time is come, they seek out some quiet,
secluded spot, make their last lair, and lay them down there to die;
unafraid they, and unashamed. Yea, the very stars in their courses,
though they glow for centuries and centuries, lose their radiance at
last; they grow cold and crumble away into cosmic ash. What are we
that we should think to escape this common destiny of all earthly
things, or resent this final blow of fate called death?"

**[And/or]**

Centuries ago the Roman philosopher Seneca wrote:

"In the presence of death, we must continue to sing the song of life.
We must be able to accept death and go from its presence better able
to bear our burdens and to lighten the load of others. Out of our
sorrows should come understanding. Through our sorrows, we join
with all of those before us who have had to suffer and all of those
who will yet have to do so. Let us not be gripped by the fear of death.
If another day be added to our lives, let us joyfully receive it, but let
us not anxiously depend on our tomorrows. Though we grieve the
deaths of our loved ones, we accept them and hold on to our memories as precious gifts. Let us make the best of our loved ones while
they are with us, and let us not bury our love with death."

*Adapted*

## Personal Reflections/Eulogy

*At this point in the service, the leader or some other designated
person—with or without the contributions of others—could speak
personally and particularly of the person for whom the memorial
service is being held.*

*(Following Eulogy, leader says:)* These, then, are a few of [our/my]
thoughts and remembrances of [_name of deceased_____].
Whether or not [I/ we] have succeeded in accurately portraying
[her/his] life, it is surely as Charles Gaines has written:

"No person can sum up the life of another. Life is too precious to be
passed over with mere words which ring empty. Rather it must
remain as it is remembered by those who loved and watched and

shared. For such memories are alive, unbound by events of birth and death. And as living memories, we possess the greatest gift one person can give another."

It is to each of you, then, that the living memories of [*name of deceased*_____]'s life are committed. To your hearts and minds go the enduring remembrances of this life. There will now be a period of [silence/ musical meditation]. I ask that each of you use these moments to remember [*name of deceased*_____] as only you can. Let us enter this meditation reverently, and with love.

*(End the meditation after 1 to 3 minutes with)* Amen.


**Readings** *(optional)*
*Several readings that seem appropriate to this particular life and death could be read. Perhaps the family has a favorite selection of scripture or poetry. Family and friends could be asked in advance to bring any readings they feel are appropriate.*

*(Introduce readings by saying:)* [We/I] have selected several readings which seem particularly appropriate on this day when we acknowledge the death and celebrate the life of [*name of deceased*_____].

*(Readings are shared.)*


**Summation**
And finally this, from the Native American Ishi people of the Pacific Northwest, who imagined that their dead spoke to them, saying:

"When I am dead, cry for me a little, think of me sometimes, but not too much. It is not good for you or your wife or husband or your children to allow your thoughts to dwell too long upon the dead. Think of me now and again as I was in life, at some moment which is pleasant to recall, but not for too long. Leave me in peace, as I shall leave you too in peace. While you live, let your thoughts be with the living."

**[And/or]**

Life is worth the living. It is good and it is beautiful, in spite of the tragedy with which it is forever beset. We glory in life, undergirded by the faith that its goodness is pervasive, that it is part of the texture of life, that it is of the essence of the nature of things. This is a profound faith, this confidence in life, more profound than we perhaps suspect, because it stands upon faith and faith alone. There is no proof for it, no objective test to support it, except the living of life itself, but this is perhaps the best test of all. And so we go on, those who have known sorrow and those who have not, strong in the faith that life is somehow good, even though we do not always understand it. We go on, no matter what befalls us, doing the right, following the true and the good. We go on, living the life we are given to live, knowing that it is a good life, however difficult it may at times seem to be. And in so living, we shall find that our faith is not false, that life is good to those who live it with serenity and fortitude.

*Duncan Howlett, adapted*

## Benediction

*(also appropriate for committal service)*

It is done. We have bid loving farewell to [*name of deceased*
_____].

[*Describe disposition of the body, e.g.*, Her/his body has been committed to the purifying flame/ the keeping of mother earth.

_____]

"Earth to earth, ashes to ashes, dust to dust."

We are profoundly glad that [*name of deceased*                    ]
lived. We are glad that we saw [her/his] face and felt the glow of [her/his] friendship and love. We cherish the memory of [her/his] words and deeds and character. Carrying [her/him] thus in our hearts, let us now go from this place in comfort and peace, assured that even in this time of loss and sorrow, life remains precious and good. May we also on this day rekindle in our hearts an appreciation for the gifts of life and other persons.

Let us honor the life of [*name of deceased*                    ]
by living, ourselves, more nobly and lovingly in the days ahead. As you return to the routines of your lives, go in great peace, dear friends, and may [God/an abiding peace] go with you. Amen.

46

# Memorial Readings for Specific Situations

## When Death Comes for the Very Aged

There is, it seems, something tenderly appropriate in the death of
the very aged. When the duties of life have all been done; when the
sun touches the horizon; when the purple twilight falls upon the
past, the present, and the future; when memory with dim eyes can
no longer easily spell the blurred and faded records of the vanished
days—then death comes like a strain of music. The road has been
long, the journey difficult, and the traveler stops at the welcoming
inn.

*Robert Ingersoll*

## When Death Comes Prematurely

Leaves should not fall in early summer. Winter should not follow on
the heels of spring. Yet when they do, we can and must speak for
life. For there is no answer to death but to live vigorously and
beautifully. We give respect and dignity to the one we mourn only
when we respect and dignify life and move toward its richest
fulfillment.

*Angus MacLean*

The morning glory that blooms for an hour
Differs not at heart
From the giant pine that lives for a thousand years.

*Zen Proverb*

## When Death Comes by Suicide

We come here bearing our grief and perhaps feeling bruised by this
death and what we might have done to prevent it. Remember that
no single act of desperation can portray a life. No matter how stalked
by hurt, this life also had its moments of delight and happiness,
caring and friendship, sharing and love. Let us be daring enough
never to forget these.

Let us admit the deep truth that none of us carries enough concern
for our brothers and sisters on this earth. We try with our best
resources, with what we can bring to bear, with what we can lavish
out of self at the time. But sometimes it may not be enough, though
our failures are not through callousness.

Self-death does not mean life denial, but it is the cry of despair for
more life. It is the refusal to crawl forever through the yawning
caverns of pain and absurdity. The battle may be long and arduous,
leaving a personal sense of alienation after an epic conflict within the

self. Whenever a death cuts across a life, we are left with a certain incompleteness. We know that [s/he] leaves much unfinished, unfulfilled, unsaid. There are yet other things we wanted to share with [her/him], and [s/he] with us. But what has been must suffice. What is and cannot be changed must be accepted. We are simply thankful that we could know and partake in the journey of life with [her/him], for it has enriched us all.

*Peter Raible*

## When Death Comes to a "Difficult" Person

And because [*name of deceased*                                                    ]
sometimes had a difficult time with life and others, this reading from Margaret Bruner:

"Say this of me, if something need be said,
when from this house of clay my soul has fled;
say that I tried,
but could not always keep the high resolve.
The road was very steep,
and often when I needed poise and strength I faltered on the last,
    hard, mountainous length.
If I had foes, I have forgiven them,
but this is worthy of no diadem.
And if by some I was misunderstood,
to these I leave a wish that all good things may be their portion.
Know for every wrong I did, I paid in agony.
In song I poured my heart's blood out to make amend.
I speak these words to kindred and friend.
Grant me compassion now that life has passed,
and pray my spirit finds peace at last."

## When Death Comes to Someone the Service Leader Doesn't Know

I share with you the agony of your grief; the anguish of your heart
    finds echo in my own.
I know I cannot enter all you feel nor bear with you the burden of
    your pain; I can but offer what my love does give: the strength of
    caring, the warmth of one who seeks to understand the silent
    storm-swept barrenness of so great a loss.
This I do in quiet ways, that on your lonely path you may not walk
    alone.

*Howard Thurman*

# A Quaker-Style Memorial Service

## Order of Service

Opening Silent Meditation
Sharing Remembrances
Closing Circle

## Checklist

Attendees notified of plans
Circle of chairs around
candle/centerpiece

Another form of memorial service which can be very meaningful and comforting is a "Quaker-style" participatory service. Such a service requires little or no formal planning as it is essentially spontaneous in nature.

One person who attended such a service described it as "the most beautiful and meaningful memorial service I ever attended" and went on to describe how such a service happens:

"In the traditional Quaker manner, all sat around in a circle with only a rug and a large candle in the center, and a number of those who knew the deceased spoke feelingly of what she had meant to them, and what she had done for other people.

"There were no rehearsed speeches, no formal eulogy by someone who had to be briefed. The testimonies were given from firsthand experience and from the heart...and at the end, all joined hands with their neighbors, in accordance with their custom."

If you decide to hold such an informal service, it is wise to inform all who will be attending of the spontaneous and participatory nature of the service, so that all can be comfortable and can collect their thoughts, remembrances, and affirmations before the event. Some may wish to write down what they will share.

The service could begin with the leader calling the group into a few minutes of reflective silence. After the sharings have seemingly run their course, with periods of silence allowed in between, the leader could ask the group to stand and hold hands in a circle, thereby bringing the service to a close.

Such a service could also begin with a pre-selected reading and end with another, in order to provide an appropriate context for the spontaneous comments of the participants.

# Committittal Service Components

*Committal services at the graveside or where the ashes are to be scattered are usually brief. In addition to the Words of Committal, you may wish to include a reading or two, a prayer, and a benediction. Or, if the committal is the only service being held, you may wish to plan a longer service; see materials in the Memorial Service.*

**Order of Service**
Words of Committal

**Checklist**
Check state/province laws re: disposition of remains.

## Words of Committal

*(For interring a body or burying ashes)*

With deep reverence, we lay the [body/ashes] of [*name of deceased* _____ ] in this hallowed ground. Here, under the wide and open sky, this child of creation will rest in peace. And we dedicate this simple place, amid these natural surroundings, to [her/his] memory. We lay [her/his body/ her/his ashes] in that gentle earth which has been humanity's chief support since we first walked beneath the sun. To the good earth and the great nature that are the source of human existence, we now give back the body of our loved one. We leave [her/him] in peace with our thoughts of love and tenderness. Thinking of [her/him] thus, let us go in quietness of spirit and live in understanding one with another. Now may [her/his] spirit abide in our hearts, even as the eternal spirit has descended upon [her/him] in benediction this day.     Amen.

**50**

*(For the scattering or burial of ashes following cremation)*

Life burns us up like a fire,
And song goes up in flame;
The body returns in ashes
To the ashes whence it came.

Out of things it rises,
And laughs, and loves, and sings;
Slowly it subsides
Into the char of things.

Yet a voice soars above it—
Love is great and strong;
The best of us forever
Escapes, in love and song.

*John Hall Wheelock*

**[Or]**

Gently, reverently, we lay these ashes away: May they lie softly in
our memories of you. No one could know how many eons and eons it
took to bring this miraculous blossoming of dust to the beauty of
you. Nor whether, if ever, in some unknown eon to come, it will
awaken again to the same unanswerable questions.

*Author unknown*

**[Or]**

It nearly cancels my fear of death, my dearest said, when I think of
cremation. To roar up in flames—I am used to it. I have flamed with
love or fury so often in my life, no wonder my body is tired, no
wonder it is dying. We had great joy of my body. Scatter the ashes....

*Robinson Jeffers*

## Chapter Five
# Readings and Meditations for Group and Formal Worship

What follows is a collection of readings and meditations you may wish to insert in addition to, or in place of, selections appearing in the services outlined in Chapters 2 through 4.

Or you may find this collection a helpful resource on special occasions in your community or within your family. There are Opening Words, Chalice or Candle Lighting Words, Meditations and Prayers, Closing Words, Table Graces, and Bedtime Prayers.

The Responsive Reading below is based on the Unitarian Universalist Principles and Purposes as stated in the Bylaws of the Unitarian Universalist Association. Use it in its entirety, or repeat the first seven principles as an affirmation of your Unitarian Universalist beliefs.

## Responsive Reading
*Read responsively with leader, or divide group into two sections and alternate.*

**All: As members and friends of this Unitarian Universalist congregation, we covenant to affirm and promote:**
The inherent worth and dignity of every person;

**Justice, equity, and compassion in human relations;**
Acceptance of one another and encouragement to spiritual growth in our congregations;

**A free and responsible search for truth and meaning;**
The right of conscience and the use of the democratic process within our congregations and in society at large;

**The goal of world community with peace, liberty and justice for all;**
Respect for the interdependent web of all existence of which we are a part.

*[Optionally, the reading could end here, or continue on next page:]*

**All: The living tradition we share draws from many sources:**

Direct experience of that transcending mystery and wonder, affirmed in all cultures, which moves us to a renewal of the spirit and an openness to the forces which create and uphold life;

**Words and deeds of prophetic women and men which challenge us to confront powers and structures of evil with justice, compassion and the transforming power of love;**

Wisdom from the world's religions which inspires us in our ethical and spiritual life;

**Jewish and Christian teachings which call us to respond to God's love by loving our neighbors as ourselves;**

Humanist teachings which counsel us to heed the guidance of reason and the results of science, and warn us against the idolatries of the mind and spirit.

**All: Grateful for the religious pluralism which enriches and ennobles our faith, we are inspired to deepen our understanding and expand our vision. As members and friends of this congregation we enter into this covenant, promising to one another our mutual trust and support.**

# Opening Words

Come into the circle of caring,
Come into the community of gentleness, of justice and love.
Come, and you shall be refreshed.
Let the healing power of this people penetrate you,
Let loving kindness and joy pass through you,
Let hope interfuse you,
And peace be the law of your heart.
In this human circle,
Caring is a calling.
All of us are called.
So come into the circle of caring.

*Richard Gilbert (adapted)*

From our fragmented personal worlds,
 we gather here to seek wholeness.
From the feeling of isolation and loneliness,
 we come here to feel connectedness.
From the vast evils in the world,
 we seek here to relate to what is good.
From the tempting idols of the mind and the confusion of the spirit,
 we would find here something of meaning.
From the proclamations of doom on every hand,
 we would find here what is hopeful.
From thoughtless non-caring,
 we would be charged here with the spirit of vital faith
 in ourselves and love for our human family.

*Source unknown*

*Service leader*:  We come together:

*Right side*:  We come together committed to search for the light
 that is right for ourselves and all other human
 beings.

*Left side*:  We come together respecting and valuing
 our differences, the differences we share
 openly and honestly.

*Right side*:  We come together in love, with respect and concern
 for selves.

*Left side*:  The selves in us and the selves in others.

All: To be the best we can be, we come together.

*From "Leading Congregations in Worship—A Guide"*

May the blessings of our fellowship be upon us in this hour and in
 the days to come:
That we may seek the truth more devotedly,
That we may think more independently,
That we may reflect more searchingly,
That we may know ourselves more completely,
That we may love more freely,
That we may forgive more quickly,
That we may pray more thoughtfully,
That we may act more courageously,
That we may live more nobly.

*Paul Carnes*

Our many different paths come together in this special place, graced by the history of our free religious heritage.

Let us be mindful of forces deep within which call us to become more than we are.

May this hour bring rest and renewal, comfort and challenge.

May we be reminded here of our highest aspirations, and inspired to bring our gifts of love and service to the altar of humanity.

May we know once again that we are not isolated beings, but that we are connected—in mystery and miracle—to the universe, to this community, and to each other.

*From "Leading Congregations in Worship—A Guide"*

# Chalice or Candle Lighting Words

Unitarian Universalist congregations are dedicated to the proposition that behind all our differences and beneath all our diversity there is a unity which makes us one and binds us forever together in spite of time and death and the space between the stars. We pause in silent witness to this unity.   (*Light flame.*)

*David Bumbaugh*

May the light we now kindle
inspire us to use our powers:
> to heal and not to harm,
> to help and not to hinder,
> to bless and not to curse,
> to serve you, spirit of freedom.

*Passover Haggadah*

In the light of truth
and the warmth of love,
we gather to seek, to sustain, to share.

*Marjorie Montgomery*

We gather this hour, as do all people of faith,
With joys and sorrows, gifts and needs.
We light this beacon of hope, sign of our quest for truth and
    meaning,
In celebration of the life we share together.

*Christine Robinson*


As the budding flower bursts into bloom,
As the glowing light kindles into flame,
May the spirit of life and love
    bloom and flame within us,
    with ever-renewing light and love.

*Source unknown*


# Meditations and Prayers

In the sacred stillness of a shared silence,
Let us listen to the wisdom of our own hearts and minds.

*From "Leading Congregations in Worship—A Guide"*


Let us seek the quiet and the calm.
Let us lay aside our loud calling.
Let us lay aside our struggle.
Speak softly:
Let us listen to the melodies that recall other proportions.
Our moments tarry not with us.
Let us then seek the dimension that endures:
    beyond all nowness and hereness,
    beyond all requirement and all particularity.
Let us speak softly that we may hear...
Let us enter into the quiet.

*Timothy Ashton*

How quiet it is when we have the patience to be silent.
How much we can learn in moments like these.
We can learn to have patience within ourselves,
    to better understand who and what we are.
We can learn to have patience with others,
    to better listen to what they say and how they feel.
We can learn to have patience with life,
    to better work with it, rather than against it.
How much we *do* need silence:
    Silence for truth so that we may learn wisdom,
    Silence for wisdom so that we may love,
    Silence for love so that we may be just,
    Silence for justice so that we may live fully.
May we be more patient and more silent,
    so that we may proceed with courage and compassion.

*Charles Gaines*


Let there be silence,
    let there be reverence in your heart.
Let all the sounds of earth flood over you,
    in order that you may receive that which only silence
    can make possible.
Drop down your burdens on the earth,
    and feel the strength of earth well up through you,
    flow upward from the ground through bone and sinew,
    into strength.
Rest your heart in silence,
    and a thousand songs you never heard before
    will pour into your ears.
Throw open the doors of your heart to all,
    and as its invitation answer finds, your heart will be full,
    and they who come will be filled as well.
Let there be silence...let there be reverence.
Let there be welcome,
    and there will be wonder in your heart.

*Robert Weston*

O our Mother the Earth, O our Father the Sky,
Your children are we, and with tired backs
We bring you the gifts you love.
Then weave for us a garment of brightness;
May the warp be the white light of morning,
May the weft be the red light of evening,
May the fringes be the falling rain,
May the border be the standing rainbow.
Thus weave for us a garment of brightness,
That we may walk fittingly where birds sing,
That we may walk fittingly where grass is green,
O our Mother the Earth, O our Father the Sky.

*A Tewa Prayer*


O Creative Spirit of Life,
We give thanks for all the blessings that are ours.
We seek strength to bear the pain that may be ours.
In our hearts, we would acknowledge our failures to keep faith with
    our sisters and brothers.
This day and every day, may we affirm the grace of all creation;
May we be ever mindful of the world's need for greater compassion,
    justice and beauty.    Amen.

*Bruce Southworth*


God of the earth and the sky and the sea and the human soul,
We thank thee for all the seasons, and for the refreshment of life and
    the incoming tide of the spirit and the harvest of our hopes and
    our deeds.
Kindle ever new hope in our hearts.
Give us courage and kindness and dreams and resolution and
    achievement.
We pray that we may minimize our weakness and magnify our
    strength and do justly and love mercy and walk humbly with
    thee.
We pray for greater understanding among all people, beginning with
    us.
We pray for patience and perseverance and faith and love.    Amen.

*Dana McLean Greeley*

Thou Infinite Spirit of Life, kindle in our hearts the spirit of love and
of understanding and of justice, and open our eyes to the
perception of thy truth.
Bind us together, and with all our beloved, as members one of
another.
And let all our worship be fruitful, in wisdom and in toil and in
trust.  Amen.

*Dana McLean Greeley*


Between the morning and the night of our desires,
Between our ideals and our accomplishments,
We would pause to reflect on the meaning of life, and especially on
the meaning of our own lives.
May we have the wisdom to see that only a few things bear the mark
of the eternal:
The giving we have invested in others;
The love we have expressed in deeds;
The work we did because we loved it;
The truth we spoke and followed;
The justice we stood for, despite the fear of consequences:
The evil we turned into good, because we saw that none of
us lives apart, but all are members one of another.
May we come to see the meaning of our days, so that we might begin
to live more deeply and more fully.
May we lift up our eyes to the holy mountain and seek the steady
stars at night.
In the quiet of the next few moments let us think on these things.
(*Silence*)
By the meditations of our hearts and the reflections of our minds,
may we be lifted up in higher resolve and greater commitment.
Amen.

*Source unkown*


# Closing Words

Be ours a religion which, like sunshine, goes everywhere:
Its temple, all space;
Its creed, all truth;
Its shrine, the good heart;
Its scripture, all wisdom;
Its ritual, works of love;
Its profession of faith, divine living.

*Theodore Parker*

And now may love hallow every home and every heart;
May the light of truth shine bright among you,
And bless you with wisdom, strength, and peace.    Amen.

*From "Leading Congregations in Worship—A Guide"*

We have been blessed this morning by who we are and by the hope
    and promise inherent in the community we can build here.
Remember that hope and promise.
Remember that you are a unique and needed part of it.
Live its beauty! Tell its story!
Go in peace. Return with light. Amen.

*John Corrado*


To those of you who came here seeking the holy,
    may the holy go with you.
To those of you who came here seeking to embrace life,
    may life return your affection.
To those of you who came here seeking a better way,
    may a way be found,
    and the courage to take it, step by step.

*Robert Doss*


Hold on to what is good,
    even if it is a handful of earth.
Hold on to what you believe,
    even if it is a tree which stands by itself.
Hold on to what you must do,
    even if it is a long way from here.
Hold on to life,
    even if it is easier letting go.
Hold on to the hand of your neighbor,
    even when we are apart.

*Adapted from the Pueblo*


Should the voyage of life bear us on separate courses,
    forget not:
    That the same stars shine over us,
    That we are warmed by the same sun,
    That we belong to the same human family,
    That the same ideals stir within our hearts,
    While we are absent from one another.

*Source unknown*

Deep peace of the running wave to you,
Deep peace of the flowing air to you,
Deep peace of the great earth to you,
Deep peace of the shining stars to you,
Deep peace to each of us gathered here today.

*Source unknown*

May the truth that makes us free,
And the hope that never dies,
And the love that casts out fear,
Lead us forward together,
'Til the day breaks and the shadows flee away.

*Source unknown*

May the blessing of truth be upon us,
May the power of love direct and sustain us,
May the peace of this community preserve our going out and our
    coming in,
From this time forth, until we meet again.

*Source unknown*

## Table Graces

May the love we share around this table with family and friends
    renew us in spirit.
May the spirit of hope, joy, peace, and love dwell within our hearts
    this day and forever more.    Amen.

■

In the light of love and the warmth of this family
We gather to seek, to sustain, and to share.

■

Spirit of Life, our family here assembled is abidingly grateful for the
    beauty of this place in which we dwell.
We are thankful also for good food to eat and the health to enjoy it,
    for the love that binds our lives and sustains our spirits.    Amen.
*Anthony Friess Perrino*

May we hold hands quietly for a moment...
Feeling love flow around us and through us,
    knowing that as we give it away
    there is always more here.

■

O God, we are thankful for this food and for all that
    nourishes us in life.
May we use them with imagination for the life of others.    Amen.

■

Bearing in mind that we live our lives at the expense of other life,
may we be worthy of the sacrifice.

*Joan Goodwin*

■

May we come to know what is good in us, to use what is good in us,
and to share what is good in us with one another.

*Donald T. Marshall*

■

A circle of friends is a blessed thing;
Sweet is the breaking of bread with friends;
For the honor of their presence at our board
We are deeply grateful.

■

It is a blessing to be.
It is a blessing to be here.
It is a blessing to be here now.
It is a blessing to be here now, together.

# Bedtime Prayers

O God, for the beauty of this day and for the gift of morning to come,
I thank you.
Give me wisdom for living tomorrow, the courage to change what I
can, and the grace to accept what I cannot change.
Bless my family and friends, and be with people everywhere in their
need.
Now I lay me down to sleep.
Help me to be free of fear, give me peace.  Amen.

*Source unknown; contributed by Burton D. Carley*


Thank you, God, for all life brings,
      for health and play and all good things.
And help me use my heart and mind
      to make me strong and keep me kind.  Amen.

*Source unknown; contributed by Burton D. Carley*


The sun has gone down and the friendly dark has come.
It is time to sleep.
Let me think over all I have done: good deeds to do again, bad deeds
to forgo and forget.
Now I shall sleep and grow while I sleep, knowing that tomorrow
will be a new day.

*Source unknown; contributed by Joyce Smith*

## Your Church at Home
## Anywhere in the World

The Church of the Larger Fellowship (CLF) provides a ministry to isolated religious liberals around the world. Our denomination's "church by mail," CLF offers a spiritual home within the Unitarian Universalist movement for individuals unable to attend a local congregation. CLF members receive regular monthly mailings and may borrow sermons, books, audio and video tapes, and lifespan religious education curricula from our extensive lending library. CLF also supports many small congregations with worship and programming resources. For more information, write or call the Church of the Larger Fellowship, 25 Beacon Street, Boston, MA 02108; (617) 742-2100.